# HOW CELL PHONES WORK

BY NADIA HIGGINS • ILLUSTRATED BY GLEN MULLALY

Published by The Child's World®
1980 Lookout Drive • Mankato, MN 56003-1705
800-599-READ • www.childsworld.com

ACKNOWLEDGMENTS
The Child's World®: Mary Berendes, Publishing Director
Content Consultant: Paul Ohmann, PhD, Associate Professor
   of Physics, University of St. Thomas
The Design Lab: Design and production
Red Line Editorial: Editorial direction

LIBRARY OF CONGRESS
CATALOGING-IN-PUBLICATION DATA
Higgins, Nadia.
  How cell phones work / by Nadia Higgins ;
illustrated by Glen Mullaly.
       p. cm.
  Includes bibliographical references and index.
  ISBN 978-1-60973-215-8 (library reinforced : alk. paper)
  1. Cell phones—Juvenile literature. I. Mullaly, Glen, 1968- ill.
II. Title.
  TK6564.4.C4H54 2012
  384.5'3--dc22                2011010914

Photo Credits © Shutterstock Images, cover, 1, 8, 24 (top
left); Arpad Benedek/iStockphoto, 4 (left); Greg McCracken/
iStockphoto, 4 (right); iStockphoto, 5 (left), 5 (center),
9, 10; Underwood & Underwood/Library of Congress, 5
(right); Shaun Lowe/iStockphoto, 6 (left); Brian Sullivan/
iStockphoto, 6 (right); AP Images, 7 (top); Darryl Sleath/
Shutterstock Images, 7 (bottom); Laurent Davoust/
iStockphoto, 11 (left), 24 (bottom left); Milos Luzanin/
iStockphoto, 11 (right), 23, 24 (center left); Don Bayley/
iStockphoto, 15; Vladimir Prusakov/Shutterstock Images,
24 (right); Rafiq Maqbool/AP Images, 25; Alex Slobodkin/
iStockphoto, 26

Printed in the United States of America in Mankato,
Minnesota.
July 2011
PA02092

ABOUT THE AUTHOR
Nadia Higgins is a children's book writer
based in Minneapolis, Minnesota.

ABOUT THE ILLUSTRATOR
Glen Mullaly draws neato pictures for kids
of all ages from his swanky studio on the
west coast of Canada. He lives with his
awesomely understanding wife and their
spectacularly indifferent cat. Glen loves
old books, magazines, and cartoons, and
someday wants to illustrate a book on How
Monsters Work!

# TABLE OF CONTENTS

# CHAPTER ONE

# CALL ME!

You have amazing news to tell your friend. But you're stuck in the backseat of a minivan. Your chances for escape are slim. What do you do?

"Hey, Mom!" you yell. "Can I use your cell phone?"

Or maybe you have your own. In the United States, 20 percent of kids between the ages of six and 11 have cell phones. That is one out of every five kids.

## TIME LINE

**AT LEAST 150,000 YEARS AGO**
Human language has emerged.

**ABOUT 1500 BC**
The first alphabet is in use.

**BY 105 AD**
Paper is invented.

**MID-1400s**
Books can be printed. Before this, they were written by hand.

**1826**
First photo is taken.

You flip open the phone and start dialing. Or, more likely, you tap the keys and text. Either way, you expect to reach your friend in an instant. But imagine that you lived 30, 100, or 1,000 years ago. How would things be different?

**1860s**
The telegraph is widely used in the United States for fast, long-distance communication.

**1877**
The phonograph, or record player, is developed. It eventually allows people to listen to recorded music.

**1878**
The first US telephones are in use.

**EARLY 1890s**
US scientist Nikola Tesla develops the ideas behind radio and other forms of wireless communication.

The first cell phone **networks** in the United States were introduced in the early 1980s. Back then, each cell phone weighed almost 2 pounds (.9 kg) and cost $4,000! Few people could afford these phones. Instead, most people used pay phones to stay in touch on the go. Doctors and other people who needed to be reached right away also used pagers. A pager would beep. The display would show the caller's phone number. Then the person who had been beeped would call the number back from a regular phone.

> That's not a phone!

> Hello? ... Hello?

| EARLY 1900s | 1936 | 1946 | 1969 | 1973 |
|---|---|---|---|---|
| Silent movies become big business in the United States. | Television broadcasts begin. | Car phones are introduced in the United States. | The earliest form of the Internet begins. | In New York City, the first public call is made on a cell phone. |

Alexander Graham Bell had invented the telephone more than 30 years earlier. But was phone service useful? Many people were not sure. Also, only the very wealthy could afford it. Most people kept in touch through visits and letters.

Alexander Graham Bell demonstrating his invention, the telephone, in 1892

**1976**
The first home computer, Apple I, is sold.

**1983**
The first US cell phone network is introduced.

**1991**
The World Wide Web allows for the Internet to spread around the world.

**1992**
The first text message is sent.

**2007**
The Apple iPhone is introduced.

Of course, the phone was not yet invented. And, even the letter was out of reach for many. Most people could neither read nor write. News spread by word of mouth. Town criers walked the streets shouting out important events of the day. Curious people eager for news from afar greeted merchants who traveled from town to town.

# THE NUMBERS

Number of people in the world in 2010: 6.9 billion

Number of cell phone subscriptions in 2010: 5 billion

Number of cell phone subscriptions in 2000: 700 million

Percentage of US citizens who use cell phones: 91

Typical daily number of texts sent by a US teenager: 100

**100 TEXTS PER DAY!**

23:52

That's a lot of texts!

Today, most people in the United States couldn't imagine their lives without their cell phones. They rely on their phones for calling, texting, taking pictures, getting directions, watching videos, and more.

# "CAN I PLEASE GET A CELL PHONE??"

In 2010, almost half of US kids ages 10 and 11 had cell phones. Experts predict that number will only go up. Is that good news? Yes and no. Cell phones let parents keep in touch with their kids.

Phones are useful for emergencies. Cell phones are also necessary if a family does not have a landline. But a cell phone can be a major distraction. Too much time on cell phones has been linked to lower grades and not enough sleep.

It's time to sleep, not text!

# SMART OR NOT?

Cell phones fall into two main categories: feature phones and smartphones. Feature phones are basic phones. They can be used for calling, texting, or playing games. Smartphones are like little computers you keep in your pocket. The keypad usually looks like a computer's keyboard. So, texting is easier. Smartphones usually connect to high-speed Internet. Users can read and write e-mails or

surf the Web on the go. Some popular smartphones are the iPhone, the BlackBerry, the Droid, and the Nexus One. More people are switching from feature phones to smartphones. By 2012, smartphones will outnumber feature phones.

*Top*: A feature phone has a numeric keypad.
*Left*: Some smartphones have a touch screen.

# CHAPTER TWO

# MESSAGE SENT...

What's the difference between calling someone on a cell phone and talking to them at the dinner table? For one, talking in person involves only sound **waves**. They travel directly from your mouth to the other person's ears.

A cell phone call begins and ends with sound waves. But other kinds of energy also play a part. The information you send—your voice, photo, or text— changes form several times along a call's path.

Please pass the pickles.

As you read this book, you are being bombarded by energy. All kinds of invisible waves are zipping by you. Some even pass through you. Many of these are radio waves, which you can't see.

Cell phones send information by radio waves. So, why don't they pick up your favorite radio station? The answer involves **frequency**. Frequency is how often a wave vibrates. Radio waves range in frequency.

The US Federal Communications Commission (FCC) sets rules about radio waves. This government agency makes sure radio waves from radios and radio waves from cell phones don't interfere with each other. Radio stations are allowed to use radio waves only within a low frequency range. Cell phones operate in a higher frequency range.

# CALL ME

What happens to your voice when you make a call? The microphone in your cell phone **translates** sound waves (your voice) into electrical signals. Here's how:

**1.** Anything that makes sound vibrates. This includes a guitar string, a pounding hammer, or your voice box. When you speak, touch your throat. You can feel your vocal cords vibrating. They move back and forth incredibly fast. When the vocal cords move outward, they push the air around them. Air gets squeezed—air **molecules** crowd together. Then, the vocal cords move inward. The air molecules spread out. So, there is a pattern inside a sound wave. One area with molecules pushed together is followed by one area with molecules spread apart. The pattern goes on and on.

When you make a call, your phone captures the pattern of your voice. Then it translates the pattern into electrical signals. The voltage, or strength of the electrical signals, varies the way the sound waves do.

**HOW DOES A PHONE TRANSLATE SOUND?**

Sound waves move outward from a source like ripples in a pond.

**2.** Next, the information in the electrical signals is turned into a code. This code is made up of only 1s and 0s. The numbers form patterns, such as 1100011 or 1110011. The possibilities are nearly endless. Millions of numbers can carry huge amounts of information.

**3.** The digital information is carried on radio waves. The digital code—the 1s and 0s—is represented by thousands of tiny pulses in the waves.

# CHAPTER THREE

# MESSAGE RECEIVED

So, how does your message then get to your friend? Radio waves carry the digital information from your phone to a tall metal tower called a base station. The tower has an antenna and other radio equipment. From there, the radio waves travel to a switching center. Here, they may be sent to a landline. Or, the radio waves may continue to another cell phone.

When your friend gets your call on her cell phone, everything happens in reverse. The digital information carried on the radio waves is translated back to electrical signals. Then the electrical signals are translated back into sound waves. Your friend hears the news you wanted to tell her!

# BASE STATION

Each base station covers a geographic area. The area is called a cell. As you move from cell to cell, your phone automatically finds the base station in the cell you are in. But cells can handle only a certain number of calls at a time. So, the size of the cell depends on how many users are inside it. A city has hundreds of cells. They are often less than a mile apart. Out in the country, one base station may serve quite a large area. If you're too far away from the base station, you may not have coverage.

# CHAPTER FOUR

# TAKE IT APART

Text and images appear on the liquid crystal display, or LCD.

You dial, text, and operate the phone through the keypad.

Sound comes through the speaker. It changes electrical signals back into your friend's voice.

You talk into the microphone. It changes your voice into electrical signals.

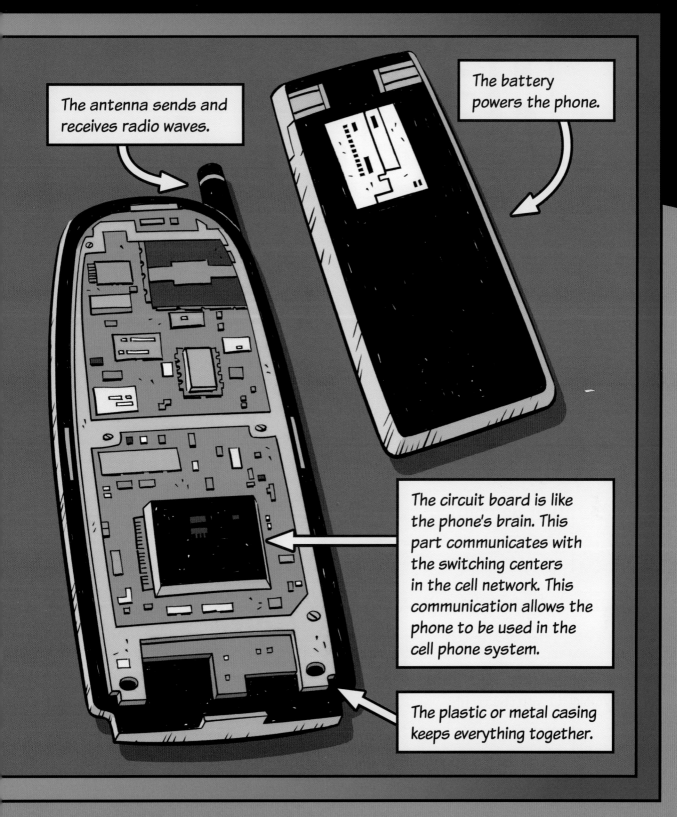

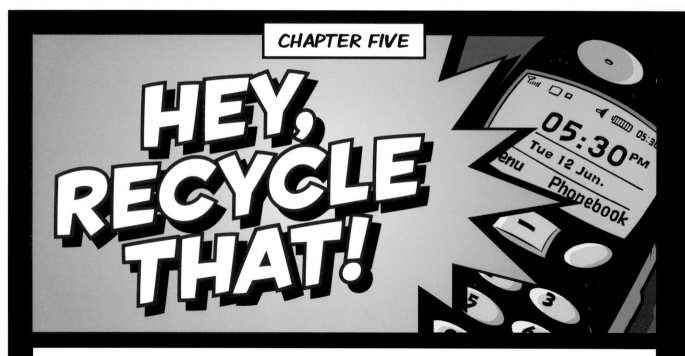

# CHAPTER FIVE

# HEY, RECYCLE THAT!

The next generation of your cell phone is coming out in a month. It has all the latest apps and looks way cooler than your phone now. You want to get it, but what do you do with your old phone?

MADE FROM 100% RECYCLED CELL PHONES

Don't trash it! Cell phones that are thrown away sit in landfills or burn up in incinerators. Both hurt the environment. Cell phones have toxic materials that could seep into the ground, water, or air.

Luckily, you can recycle your phone. Cell phones are recycled in two ways. They can be sent to special centers where they are stripped of personal information. Then the phones are resold. Or, the phones are sent to special factories. There, metals and other materials are removed. Some materials are reused in other products.

## A SHORT LIFE

*Cell phones are constantly being upgraded. Old models are quickly replaced. The average life of a cell phone is just one and a half years! About 500 million old cell phones are collecting dust in homes or filling landfills in the United States. Fewer than 2 percent of old cell phones are recycled.*

# CELL PHONES FOR SOLDIERS

Cell Phones for Soldiers is a charity that will gladly take your old cell phone. US soldiers stationed overseas reuse the phones.

Old phones are accepted at 40,000 drop-off locations around the country. Phones can also be mailed for free. To find out how to donate your phone, visit the Web site of Cell Phones for Soldiers.

# CHAPTER SIX

# UPDATES

Cell phones have changed the very basics of how we communicate. Teenagers no longer talk on the phone as much as their parents did. The majority of teens now text their friends rather than call them. How else are cell phones changing our world?

## Help in Developing Countries

In some poor countries, people are more likely to have cell phones than electricity or running water. Often, it's actually cheaper and easier to create a cell network than other basic services.

Cell phones offer unique ways of helping developing nations. Citizens of those countries can use their phones to:

- Keep up-to-date on news that would otherwise be unavailable.
- Find important health information. For example, they could find out when vaccines are arriving at a nearby clinic.
- Learn how to read.
- Learn English.
- Voice opinions about the government. For example, monks in the Asian country of Myanmar used their phones to get on Twitter. There, they expressed outrage at some of their government's actions.

# SAVE A TRIP

In many developing countries, up to 66 percent of people live in rural areas. However, most doctors and clinics are in the cities. Sick people have to travel to the city for health care. This can take time and money they may not have. New cell phone software can help prevent needless trips to doctors. People send in their symptoms and necessary pictures by phone. They communicate with their doctors before making the long, expensive trip. Sometimes a trip is not even needed.

## Saved by Cell Phones

You know that cell phones are handy to have in an emergency. You can easily call for help if you're lost, locked out, or hurt. But even if you can't talk to rescuers, your cell phone can help them find you.

One South Carolina woman was lucky that she had her cell phone on a walk. She stopped to look at a creek close to her home. Suddenly, the ground crumbled beneath her. She fell and landed on the creek bank. The woman was able to call 911 on her cell

phone. She then fell unconscious and was unable to speak. Rescuers could hear her breathing, though. They used the GPS system in her phone to track her down. A sheriff found her, and the woman lived.

## Don't Be Rude, Dude!

Don't eat with your mouth full. Don't interrupt. Don't forget to say "please." You learned about manners long ago. But cell phones have added more manners to know.

- **Turn it off.** At school, restaurants, and theaters, turn off your phone or put it on vibrate. Nobody wants to hear someone's phone ringing just as the aliens are about to attack in the movie.

- **Call back later.** If you're hanging out with a friend, let the call go to voicemail. Or, tell the caller that you'll call back later. Your friend will feel like your time together is important to you.

- **Step outside.** If you must answer a phone call, excuse yourself and talk outside. Most people don't like listening to other people's phone conversations.

## Watch Out!

Kids playing, bikes zipping by, squirrels scurrying. . . . Drivers already have to deal with so many distractions. Cell phones add another one. Drivers talking on cell phones are four times more likely to cause a crash than those who are not. Drivers who text are 23 times more likely to crash.

What can drivers do? They can pull over to take an important call. They can use a headset so their hands stay on the wheel. Or they can just let the call go to voicemail. Those simple actions could prevent an accident!

# IT'S 2100!

What will a cell phone look like in a few decades? They might have cool features, like these:

- **3-D imaging:** A 3-D image of your favorite photo floats above the screen.
- **Biodegradable materials:** Your phone could break down in a landfill, just like an apple core.
- **Solar power:** Batteries no longer power your phone. Instead, the sun powers it.
- **Bendable materials:** Your phone could bend around your wrist, like a bracelet.
- **Tiny size:** Your cell phone could be small enough to fit inside your ear.

# I SPEAK I.M.

Sending text messages as full words or sentences takes a long time. That's why texting uses shortened phrases that save time—and thumb cramping. Here are a few common ones:

NMU: not much, you?

LOL: laugh out loud

C U L8R: see you later

IDK: I don't know

## WORDS TO KNOW

**frequency** (FREE-kwun-see): Frequency is how often a wave vibrates, or moves back and forth. Sound waves have a different frequency from radio waves.

**landline** (LAND-lyn): A landline is a phone that needs a telephone cable, as opposed to a cell phone. A home phone is a landline.

**molecule** (MOL-uh-kyool): A molecule is the most basic unit into which a substance can be broken down. A molecule is made of two or more atoms.

**network** (NET-wurk): A network is a group of things that is connected to each other. A cell phone network allows people to make and receive calls on their cell phones.

**translate** (TRANS-layt): To translate means to make understandable in a different way or language. Cell phones translate sound waves into electrical signals.

**waves** (WAYVS): Waves are vibrations of energy. Sound and radio are two types of waves.

## FIND OUT MORE

Visit our Web site for links about how cell phones work: childsworld.com/links

Note to Parents, Teachers, and Librarians: We routinely verify our Web links to make sure they are safe and active sites. So encourage your readers to check them out!

## INDEX